Thoughts From My
Heart

Thoughts From My Heart

Inspired By The True Inner Beauty

That Every Woman Has

KENNY GABLE

authorHOUSE®

AuthorHouse™
1663 Liberty Drive
Bloomington, IN 47403
www.authorhouse.com
Phone: 1-800-839-8640

First published by AuthorHouse   01/27/2012

ISBN: 978-1-4685-2956-2 (sc)
ISBN: 978-1-4685-2955-5 (ebk)

Library of Congress Control Number: 2011962584

Printed in the United States of America

Contents

In My Mind

Just when I think your smile can't get any more beautiful, you take the light from the stars that shine at night, and release them in my eyes, just with a simple movement of your lips. Just when I think my life has set up barriers to confine your touch, you breach those barriers with a simple touch of your love that crosses those boundries causing my life to crave you daily. Then in my mind, when I finally think life cannot get any more wonderful, you walk over to me with those eyes, and then run through my heart and soul, leaving your beautiful love, for me to follow, to your heart, where you are waiting fervently for me.

You Blessed My Life

When you grabbed my hands, I was startled. When you grabbed my shoulders and pulled me closer, I was surprised. When your lips grabbed mine and you mystified my life with just one look from your eyes, it was my soul that was enamoured. Then after saturating my heart with visions of eternity and euphoria, it was my life that had just been blessed.

The Vessel

A woman is the vessel GOD uses to bring a child into this world, because of the qualities that she possesses. So as men, we should love and respect our women more. Because to hurt a woman, is the same as destroying what GOD has created with his own hands.

You Don't Have To

You don't have to say a word, for me to know you love me. You don't have to do a thing for me, to show me your love. You don't have to be near me, to show me affection. Because you have done all these things by coming into my life.

Once In A Lifetime

You reach out to me with your eyes, while stealing my heart, with your kiss. Leaving me with a once in a lifetime chance, to make my dreams come true.

Your Kiss

Your kiss inspires my soul so deeply, and grips my heart so firmly, that I want to write your name, in the sand that surrounds our island of paradise.

Taste Of Perfection

Your beauty is persuasive, within my sight. Your power to satisfy is prevalent throughout my life. And your touch is undeniable, as my emotions clamour for another taste of perfection, from your arms

Love Your Kiss

I love kissing you, because when we are done, I can go through my life, with your sweetness on my lips, and enjoy the taste of your love, anytime I want.

Your Eyes

Your eyes pierce the constant darkness of my soul, while your lips tantalize my heart, engulfing my life with intoxicating pleasure that electrifies my every thought.

You Are

You are from head to toe, very beautiful, very sexy, very talented, very intriguing, very alluring, magnetically attractive, superior in all ways to other women, and also the woman who now, holds my heart in her hand.

When I Want To Show Love

When I think of love, I look in your eyes.
When I speak of love, I hold you in my
arms. When I want to show love I pull you
in to my embrace, and kiss you deeply.

Our Time Together

Do not think of the time that has passed, before
we were together. Think of the time that we will
have, since we have come together.

Near You

When I am near you, my emotions tingle, my
knees get weak, and I can hear my heart scream
for me to reach out and hold you.

When You Speak My Name

When you speak my name, you paint the
most beautiful and everlasting picture,
on every wall in my life.

Always With You

When you are alone, close your eyes, and feel my love curled around you. Keeping you safe from all loneliness and unwanted feelings. Also know that my hands are holding you gently, so that you do not tremble, and you feel safe. So even though you feel alone, while I am away, know that I will always be with you, loving you.

Given To My Life

You are the inspiration for my words. You are the attraction in my eyes. You are the delicacy to my lips. You are the wonderment throughout my mind. You are the fountain of youth in my heart. You are the beauty and amazement in my life, and have given to my life, perfection.

Now You Are Loved

I see you in a fog of confusion mixed with uncertainty. I see your eyes, and they are searching for something or someone to hold on to, to ease the pain. I see you reaching out, wanting to be pulled from what you think is reality, because that is the only world, you have known, thus far. So as I am walking, I am speeding up, to get to you quicker. As I get to you, I grab your hand, and pull you from your world, into my world, which leaves you astounded, because now you are loved, and safe.

Making My Dreams Come True

You tell me you love me, by the language your body speaks. You show me you love me, by the closeness of your body. You give me your love, by making my dreams come true.

For Eternity

Every time we kiss, your love seems to flow from our lips, and flood my heart. Leaving me steep and soaked, in your love, for eternity.

I Stutter

Sometimes when we are together, I stutter my words, but that is only because my heart is busy skipping a beat

In My Past

The legend of your beauty is true, and I see it every time I close my eyes, and look with my heart. The allure of your sensuality is strong, because my body vigorously yearns for your touch, every time you inch near to me. The cries from my dreams and desires have been answered, every time you kiss me, appeasing all that has been unsatisfied, in my past.

Always Enjoy

I always enjoy seeing the temptation in your eyes, and touching the desire on your lips.

Do The Math

Let's do some math. Take two people in love, add two sets of lips. Add one kiss, take away a lifetime of pain, and add an eternity of happiness, and what do you get? One happily complete man, with the woman of his dreams, in his life.

Blindfolded

You are blindfolded by your need to see love, so I have come to rip that blindfold off of your eyes. Showing you, that you were meant for me, and I for you.

Bedtime

Bedtime is never complete until I have kissed every star in your eyes, and felt the sunset through a kiss, from your lips.

Believe Me

You are my strength, my wisdom, my night and day, my love, and my life. So when I tell you that I love you, can look inside my life, and believe me.

A Million Miles

I would walk a million miles and not worry about getting tired, if it meant I was one step closer, to getting a kiss from you.

Path To Paradise

Last night with you forged my path with glorious intentions. Your spirit is my guide, leading me and all that I am, to you and all that you are, which in my eyes, is paradise.

Book Of Dreams

Lets close the door, light the candles, turn on some music, warm the oils, and begin to write another chapter, in our book of dreams.

Every Moment Of Our Eternity

The woman every man searches for is you. The kiss every man desires upon his lips, you can give. The arms that every man yearns to feel, you have. While they keep searching,we will keep enjoying, every moment of our eternity.

I Knew

I knew it would happen sooner or later, your beauty would escape my eyes, and drift into the world, for all to see. I knew that with looks like yours, men would see you, and fight over you. Your beauty and intelligence, would split nations, causing them to go to war, thinking, the prize would be you. I knew that, sooner or later, you would be the drug of choice for so many. I knew that, your walk, would turn heads, and make beggars out of grown men. Your smile, would illuminate, all those dark places, where love used to be, but now is dark and empty. With just one touch, from you, men would sell all that was valuable, to be able to follow, hoping again to be touched. You just cannot imagine, or understand, the depth of your beauty, and the effect it has on man. And I am not talking just one man, but I am telling you, it is all men.

It Does Not Matter

It does not matter to me what you are wearing, as long as you are wearing it for me. It does not matter to me if your hair is a mess, as long as I am the one who gets to mess it up. It does not matter if you have no make-up on, because I love the woman underneath the make-up. Even your body weight does not matter, because I am not in love with your body, it is your heart that matters to me. Because your body is the chest, which holds the treasure of your heart, anything else beside your heart, does not matter.

Give Me

Give me your tears, I will give you a kiss. Give me your sorrows, I will give you an infinite amount of love. Give me you tattered up heart and I will mend it with, strings from my soul, and fill it up, with love from my heart.

Will You

Will you let me, be in your life? Will you let me, kiss away your tears, and hug away your worries. Will you let me be there, when you are sick, and then let me love you back to health. Will you let me, look deep into your river of blue eyes that leads to the waterfalls of your soul. Will you let me, climb the ladder to your heart, and clean the windows that keeps so much goodness from shining through. Will you let me pull you close, and share those soft, sweet lips, that can and have controlled minds. Will you let me, just take you from a world, full of disappointment and heartaches, and run through my life, where you are queen, and tears are outlawed. Will you let me, just take you, as you are, and live a lifetime, of ecstasy, and paradise.

Describing You

Your love is like a spirit I want to inhale. Your words are like music notes that my heart uses while composing a symphony. Your look is like a magnet that pulls souls, toward you. And your body is like a bridge, because it connects your heart to mine.

Can't Hide

You can't hide that smile, it engulfs the sun. You can't hide how deep your heart is, it goes deeper than the ocean. And as for me, I can't hide my love for you, it reaches the four corners of the earth, and reaches the highest, of all mountains.

Your Life

Your look is intense but yet intriguing. Your scent is innocent but yet delectable. Your touch is firm but yet needful. Your hold is wanted. Your body is addictive. Your kiss is hot and satisfying. And your life is important and wanted by me.

Distance

The distance from your heart to mine, is very short. The distance from your lips to mine, is very short. The distance between your body and mine, is very short. The distance in our lives for anything is very short, because we are now, bonded as one.

My Everything

If I haven't told you lately, you are my everything, you are. You are so beautiful, that I am scared to sleep some nights, for fear of missing one moment, of not seeing you. I sometimes watch you in your sleep, just to see which way, your beautiful body will turn. I love to watch you smile, and see those beautiful lips, as you smile. I am attracted, to not only the woman on the outside, but the woman on the inside, that brings your beauty to light. I love everything about you, and want to find those things, that I have missed. You are my everything, my better half, and my end to a lifetime of searching. I feel now, that I have not just found my better half, but a beginning, to a new life. Closing the door, to a troubled past.

All Of You

What is it about you, that just sizzles my emotions? Is it your walk, your smile, your eyes, your words, your lips, or just the way you look at me? There are so many things, that I can't choose, just one thing, I love all of you. Every time that we are together, I feel an emotional overload, and the only thing to stop this from happening, is for you to grab me, hold me, and kiss me. I love your kisses, and how they reach all the way, to the depths of my soul. When you look at me, I feel as though you have shrunk me, and stuck me into a new home, I call your heart. When you hold me, I turn to jelly, and am yours to spread, all throughout your life. You, must understand, that I have seen beautiful, but when these two eyes, found you walking my way, it was as if, I had just seen beauty, at its best. I thought to myself, I have seen, what men talk about, searching for. But when you came up to me, and I heard you speak, I was then under your control, and my emotions, soon followed. So when you ask me, what it is about you that I love, I will tell you all the time, it is not just one thing, but all things.

I See Us

When I look at you, I see us. I see us together for eternity. I see two people that have searched, but found no-one, but then by chance, found each other. I do see two people, growing old together. I see us having competitions with each other, on who can love each other the most. I see two people, lying together, on a blanket, under the moon and stars, telling one another, why they fell in love. Smiling the whole time, giggling like two teens, on a date for the first time. I see us walking around the lake, at night, just to watch, the lights from the stars above, twinkle in each other's eyes. I see two people embracing every wrinkle, and kissing each one, as it comes upon us. Because that means that we are growing old with each other. I see us loving the grey that grows in our hair. Because that means, that we are paying attention to and loving each other, even though, we are growing older. I see us together, on our front porch, and watching the stars above. Neither of us are looking for a shooting star, because we have no need for wishes, as our wishes came true, many years ago. I see us, still loving one another, nurturing our needs, and satisfying our wants. I see us, holding one another, at times, all night long, because we still love how the other one feels, in our arms. Actually I see us, together till our last breath. And if we were to pass on from this life, at the same time, we would do it, in each other's arms, and smiling through the whole thing.

Realize

You really must be honest with yourself. You have to realize, that when you walk by a crowd, all the men want to be with you, and the women despise you because of your magnetic, hypnotizing attractiveness. You have to realize, that when you speak, it is like some kind of love potion, let loose on the minds of men, accelerating the insaneness it causes. Clouding their minds, and pulling them by their fantasies. You have to realize, that what you possess is special, and no one else can even come close. You have what every woman desires, every woman wants, every woman needs. That is what I call, natural attraction, and the power to bring men to their knees. You have to realize, that with the power that you have, should be outlawed, but who would outlaw it, when they too, would fall in the same path, that have held so many men hostage, by their own hearts. You have to realize, that you are one of a kind, and will always be chased after by all men. So if you ever think that you are not special, and just ordinary, then all you have to do is speak, and watch how men, fall to their knees, begging to be the one that you choose.

Your Name

I noticed you, because of the twinkle, that glimmered from your eyes. I saw you turn around, and your smile lit up the whole room. As you turned, I seen your hair, as it fell on your shoulders. I was bedazzled, from the voice, I was hearing. My curiosity, crept up on me, and so I humbly went over, just to be in the presence, of someone so truly, beautiful. I asked your name, and you said, the wind says your name everyday, and the birds sing of you, and the flowers in the field, take time to honour you, before they bloom. I thought for a minute, and said, your name must be, BEAUTIFUL, and you said yes.

Will You Believe

I have exhausted all efforts and have run out of words, trying to tell you, and to get you to understand, that you are beautiful. So I will let the birds of the air, fly to you, and sing of your beauty, and then maybe you will begin to understand. I will let the flowers of the world, congregate around you, blooming at your feet, then maybe you will begin to understand. I will let music from the wind, as it blows through the air, sing its song of beauty, as it honours you. I will even let, the stars align, and the moon smile, while you are standing under them, to try and make you understand, just how beautiful you are. Will you then understand, or will you still not believe. Only you, and that beautiful heart, will have to make that decision, as to when or if you will ever believe, what I see everyday, and that is, you are truly, beautiful.

Eyes

Are those eyes as magnetic, and alluring as I have heard? Can they really, pull the thoughts, and desires from men's hearts, and bring them to the light, so that you really know, what it is they truly want. Can your eyes, really turn the direction of a crowd, from where they were going, to following you, on the path, that you are travelling? Do your eyes, pierce the thoughts of men, giving them hope, where hope never existed before? Can you turn a man's steel heart, into one of clay, and then giving you the advantage, of molding it, into the heart you have always wanted? Do your eyes magnetize, manipulate, transform, soothe, and hypnotize, whenever you want them to, and to whoever you want? Are your eyes really, powerful enough to congregate in a man's heart, and turn him selfish, for never wanting to share you with anyone? I have heard, all the stories, all the myths, all the men talking, but I am halfway around the world, but even there, I hear of your eyes.

You Do Not Realize

Do you not realize what you do to me, when we are together? You take my feelings and emotions by their hands, and run through the fields of my desires, stopping only when you feel like it. Sometimes, you even swap, the tears you have squeezed from memories of my past, and fill them with your love, so that I no longer, remember, why they rolled down my cheek. After a little bit of running, and some time spent, gazing at all the memories and visions, I have in my mind of you, you start walking again. You then start walking through the plains of my heart, still amazed, of how one man can have so much love, for one woman, but I then remind you, you are not just a woman. I keep telling you, that you are the woman, the only woman, that I care to think about. You are the only woman in my life, and the only woman I want in my life. Sometimes, I wake up, and wait til I see you smile, then that is when I know the sun has come up, I tell you again, you have done this to me. At night, I wait till I see that sparkle in your eyes, and it is then, that I know the sun has set, and I am looking at the reflection, from the stars, through your eyes. You do allot of things to me that you have no idea that is being done. At times, you can turn me inside out, just to be closer to my heart. Then at times, you have me running home from work, just to feel how beautiful you really are, and to see, you smile at me. You do more than you know to me, but there are some things, that I like to keep to myself, just so I can be reminded, that you are real, and not just a mirage

Your Words

When we are together, and you speak to me, it seems as though, I am hearing a symphony. The notes you speak, soothe my soul. When I close my eyes, I feel this overwhelming calm, take control of all tensions in my life, and run with them, until, there are no more. I see my heart fluttering, and smiling, because of the sweet music, I am hearing as you speak to me. I can feel my soul, reaching out to my heart, as if trying to get it to dance. When I look again, I do see them dancing. I then sit and watch as they, are doing so many. They waltz, they foxtrot, they tango, they two-step, and as you speak more and more in my ear. Then they get happy, and begin to break dance, and this is when I know, your words, have taken root, inside me. When you speak, your words are used to inspire the sun setting. When you speak, your words set in motion, all romance, as the sun sets, and all moments that come after it has set. To say the least, your words, are harmonic, and romantic, at the same time.

Shadows

The sun is down, and I see that our shadows, have followed us inside. They are following us, as we stroll around the house. As we are touching, and exploring, and feeling, they are doing the same. As we turn to kiss, as we turn to taste each other's thoughts, I feel them doing the same. I see one shadow leading the other, and the other shadow, following. So I think we should follow them, just to see, where they are going. As we are following, I notice, that they are going the same way, as we are going. Their path has already been determined, by the thoughts in our heads. We already knew, where we were going, when we came in. But we love one another so much, that our shadows, were so happy, to be together, that they decided to start the night before we did. I feel, the more we become as one, then we will not have to follow, our shadows, our shadows will follow us.

FAIRY TALE LOVE

I know that we don't live in a fairy tale, but where we do live, you are loved and adored, more than you could ever read about. I know that you don't have glass slippers, or dresses that capture the imagination, but what you do have, captures my imagination, and brings my fairy tales to light. Because whatever you do wear, you make beautiful, and mystify the mind. I know you don't ride in a beautiful carriage, but what you do ride in, you make all around you seem like they are in a fantasy land. You may not be queen of a land, and live in a castle. But the place you do live in is yours, and all people around you, love you, deeply, and truly. So you see, you may not live in a fairy tale, but the love you see in those fairy tales, are the exact love, you live everyday.

Always Thinking

As I wake, the thoughts about you, follow me. I think of the sun rising, and that's when you get up. I think about being the happiest man, in this world, because I see you beside me. I think of all the bad this world has to offer, and then I laugh. Because I know, you and all that you mean to me, will be at home, ready to greet me, and that is why I have the advantage. I think of all the men around me, who are sad, and not as lucky as I, and I smile. I do not smile, because of their misfortunes, but rather smile, because they have not experienced, the kind of eternal love, you have given to me. I always think to myself, no matter what happens through the day, good or bad, you always change the outcome of my day. If it is a bad day, you dissipate all evil. If it is a good day, you take it to the next level. So yes, from the time I get up, til the time, I get to come home, and fall in your arms, I am always thinking of you.

I Am Here

When you are crying, look to your heart, and know, that I am there. I am that man, absorbing your tears, so you will forget why each tear was shed, and will never shed them again.

You

It is said, beauty is in the eye of the beholder. So I tell them, beauty is not only in my eye, but in my arms, and that beauty would be you

You Always

Your eyes hold my attention, while grabbing my heart. Your words, bedazzle my imagination and reshape my thoughts. Your touch feeds the flames of my desires, while soothing my pain. You always seem to satisfy all things, within, this body.

Know Not

You know not where I come from. You know not my name. But you do know my soul, my intentions, and where I am going. So when I get to that place, in your heart, you can give me the name, you want to hear. Because, you will feel me everyday.

Are You Sure

Are you sure it is safe to go into the world? Are you sure the waters of scepticism have receded, and assurance has now started to take place. Are we totally in agreement, that it will now be two hearts, two hands, two souls twisted together, as one. I know you may be sure, but I can still see reflections from the pain, that flooded my life. So it is only natural, I tread lightly.

If I Ever

If I ever have to write about my love for you. I will write it in the sky for all to read. If I ever have to run, to prove my love for you. I will run to the sun and back. If I ever want people to hear about my love for you. I will climb the highest of all mountains, and shout, for all ears to hear.

A Place For You

If you ever feel the need to escape, to a place, where you are loved. Then come to my mind and heart. It will be there, for you to come, and to serve you love, day and night.

Everything About You

Everything about you is beautiful. From your toes to the hair on your head. Everything from your heart to your soul, and in between, is beautiful. Everything from the twinkle in your eyes, to the shape of your shadow, is beautiful. To me, in my eyes, you are beautiful.

On My Mind

So you want to know what's on my mind? Well it is simple, it is the same thing that is in my heart. It is the same thing, that makes my heart skip a beat. I will tell you, it is YOU, and YOU only

I Can Give You

I can't give you the wealth of this world, but can give you my heart. I can't give you bruises and heartaches, but I can give you, my love and affection. I can't give you lies, but I can give you truth. I don't want to give you, just this moment, I want to give you, eternity.

When I Look Around

You are the light, that shines in my life. You are the passion, I feel when we kiss. You are the security, I feel in my life. You are the memories, that we make each night. You are the right, when I have gone wrong. You are the sexy, when I need to feel like a man. You are the beautiful, when I look at you. You are the better half, when we come together. You are the everything, when I look around my life.

Everything Needed

You are the life that runs through my veins. You are love that fills my heart. You are the masterpiece that I marvel at. You are my comfort, when the world is negative. You are the positive, when all fails. You are the half of me that is the strongest. You are the part of my life that I cannot do without. You are the embodiment, of everything needed in my life

Loved You

I loved you, when you thought you were unlovable. I loved you, when you didn't love your reflection in the mirror. I loved you, when you thought no-one else would love you. I loved you, when you needed love. I loved you, after you thought everything about you, was a waste of time. I loved you, after you gave up hope. I loved you, because I wanted you to know, that my search for someone to love, was over. I loved you then, but now, holding you, I love you even more.

Silent Storm

When I look in your eyes, I feel a storm raging, and ready to conquer, all in its path. When I kiss your soft lips, I feel lightning has just struck, and feel the electricity, running through my body. When I get pulled in your arms, I feel safe and sheltered, from the storm. When we decide to take the next step further, I feel as though, you are ready to unleash, all of the passion that comes with your silent storm.

Key To Paradise

That moment of paradise transpired, and
became true, the moment our eyes, led
us to that blissful kiss, which we now call,
the key to paradise.

IF I

If I told you that I do need you, I would pull
you close, and talk to your heart. If I told you
that my search was over, I would keep holding
you, and whisper to your soul. If I told you that
I was ready for an eternity with you, I would
keep holding you, and let your life know,
through a kiss from our lips.

The Most Important Woman

It does not matter if my eyes are open, or they are closed, you are the most beautiful woman, in my eyes. It does not matter if I become rich, or I stay the same, you are the most important woman, in my life. It does not matter if the sun comes up or the stars come out, you will always be the most important woman, in my life.

You Have Asked Me

You have asked me, what do you have to do, to prove that you love me. You have to do no more, than than tell me through a kiss, from those addictive lips.

You Have Given

YOU ASKED WHAT HAVE YOU DONE TO ME. YOU HAVE GIVEN MY DREAMS TO ME. YOU HAVE FILLED THE EMPTINESS, AND VOIDED MY PAIN. YOU HAVE EXPANDED MY HEART, WITH YOUR OVERWHELMING LOVE. YOU HAVE GIVEN TO ME, WHAT NO-ONE ELSE COULD, AN EVERLASTING LOVE.

When You

When you look at me, I feel lucky. When you talk to me, I feel chosen. When you touch me, I feel relieved. When you kiss me, I feel overcome. When you hold me, I feel eternity.

Build A Bridge

How about you and me, take the love
we have for each other, and build a
bridge to, eternity.

Why I Smile

You ask me why I smile so much, well it is because, I love
you and everything about you. I love your hair, draped
over my shoulders, as we share a kiss. I love the spark in
your eyes, as you turn, and look in my eyes. I love the way
my heart skips and dances, when you grab my hand, to
bring me closer. I even love how you can turn my world
around, with just three words. I also love, the fact that I
am there with you, when the sun rises, and when the sun
sets. I just really love you, for being you.

Your

Your love, endless. Your smile, magnetic. Your eyes, penetrating. Your touch, fulfilling. Your heart, sought after. Your life, valuable. Your words, soothing and satisfying.

Could Talk

I could talk about your beauty all day long, but I would prefer to hold you for eternity. I could talk about the magical storm that brews inside those eyes of yours, but prefer to jump directly, in the storm. I could talk about spending a lifetime with you. But prefer eternity.

Wishing

I am wishing the world away, so that we can be together, without interruption. I am wishing for a shooting star, so that I can catch it, and you will have whatever you wish for. I am wishing for a kiss from you, so that my heart can grow, and feed my life, with the nourishment to live.

Waiting Eagerly

When you look in my eyes, you can see my heart and soul coexisting. Anxiously waiting for your next touch. Waiting for that rush of passion. Waiting eagerly to pull your words, inside, so they will live for eternity.

In Your Arms

I have seen paradise, through your eyes.
I have tasted perfection, from your lips. I
have experienced utopia, in your arms.

First Kiss

I want to turn back the hands of time,
so we can have our first kiss again.
I want to record the song that was
playing, during our first kiss. I want to
bottle up, that first I love you, so I will
have it everyday. I just want to take that
moment in time, when we had our first
kiss, and record it, to watch everyday.

Devote This Night

As our shadows start to merge with the night, we have given to the day, not let us take from the night. Let us take one another, and delve into those feelings, that we have been fighting all day, needing to be unleashed. Let us hold one another, and watch the world disappear. Let us devote, this night, to one another, and love all that has been neglected.

Don't Need

I don't need the sun to shine, because I have your smile. I don't need to be rich, because I have your heart. I don't need to see the stars shine, because I see the twinkle in your eyes. I don't need the world, because you are my world, and I am very happy.

I Have Kissed You

I have kissed you, and rode the waves of excitement,
through your eyes, all the way to your heart, leaving
me to revel, in all the pleasures of your love.

Worth Living

After spending one moment looking in your eyes,
I see the woman that would make eternity, worth
living.

Through My Lips

While I am kissing you, ask me through your eyes, if this kiss is the best that I have ever had, and I will answer you, through my lips.

Found The Treasure

Many men journey through the mountains, and fall short of the treasure. Some men journey through the seas, and fall short of the treasure. Some men journey through the skies, and fall short of the treasure. I journeyed through your eyes to your heart, and found the treasure.

Needing Another Kiss

Your kiss covered my heart and soul, with an umbrella of comfort, protecting my emotions from all harm. It shielded me from uncertainty that may stem from this worlds disappointments. It secludes the joy from the sorrow, leaving me ecstatic, and needing another, kiss.

With Every Heartbeat

I could kiss you, every time my heart beats, and never wear-out my lips.

From Above

There is only one thing for sure in this world, you and the beauty you possess. There is only one consistent that happens, and that is your willingness to share it with me. Then there is the only gift that keeps giving, and that is you, because you were given to me, from above.

I Love You Because

I don't love you because of the way you walk, I love you because of where you are walking to, and that is into my heart. I don't love you because of the words you speak, I love you because of who you are telling that you love, and that is me. I don't love you because of the life you have, I love you because of who you are sharing that life with, and that is me.

I Am Always Thinking Of You

I have a new name for your beauty, and it is, fiery. I also have a new name for your touch, and it is, enthralling. I have a new name for your body, and it is, scrumptious. I have a new name for your needs and desires, and it is, fulfilled. So the next time one single thought enters your mind of me never thinking of you, let it pass on through, because I am always thinking of you.

When I

If I could change your name, I would change it to beautiful. When I look at you, all I see is the beautiful woman that, turns my life inside out, leaving me a better man, than I was before I saw you. When I hold you, I feel my life getting better because my heart and soul, tells me so. When I kiss you, my emotions tangle with my desires, just to share the same feelings of ecstasy. So whether it is day or night, just being in your presence, gives way to a transformation, that makes my life feel as beautiful, as you look. So when I see you by my side, I know then that, my life has been truly blessed.

A Good Night

A good night with you would be, making it home to you safely, looking into your eyes as I say I love you, and curling up beside you with you in my arms, and going to sleep listening to your heartbeat, as it sings, I LOVE YOU

Words That You Speak

The sensations I feel come from looking in your eyes. The power I feel, comes from your kiss. The security I feel, comes from the way you hold me. The lifetime of satisfaction I feel, comes from those words that roll over those lips of perfection, and fills my heart.

I Accept

You hunger, and I feed. You question, and I answer. You ask, and I tell. You come closer, and I get weak. You offer, and I take. You love, and I love back. You wander throughout my body, and I smile. You speak to me, and my body listens. You offer eternity, and I accept.

Forever

I could call you, and tell you that I love you, but I would rather hold you in my arms, and as you feel my heart beat, with your soul, I can look upon your beautiful face, as my eyes tell you one million times over, I love you completely and unconditionally, forever.

Every Drop

Every drop of love that you squeeze from my lips is yours, and you can use it to warm your body, and feed your desires, anytime you need and want to feel, loved.